Please Poke the Bear!

a Church Story

by

Larry A. Yff

CHAPTERS

INTRODUCTION

3

Let's keep it simple from the beginning and start off with a short list:

1. Bear. That is a term that refers to aggressive action or it could literally mean the huge, 4-legged animal that we call "bear."

2. Bearings. "To get your bearings" is a term that means "you need to find your direction" or in other words, "you need to get your shit together."

What does all that have to do with this book? Everything. The church is like a sleeping bear that is content to sleep. If you wake a bear from its' sleep, it will kill you and eat you. That's why there is a phrase that says, "Please *don't* poke the bear!"

In this case, I am saying the Church is like a sleeping bear that *needs* to be woken up. It has been in hibernation for the last 400 years or so and it's time to wake up!

WAKE UP, CHURCH!!! It's time to show off your 3-inch fangs and 4-inch claws! Or maybe it's 4-inch fangs and 3-inch claws. Either way, it's time! It's time to flex all those muscles in your powerful body! It's time to wreck some shit!

Since nobody seems to want to wake it up, I figured I would. I will metaphorically poke the church so it can unleash its' fury, frustration, anger, influence and power on the world in such a way that when Jesus sees Satan and all his buddies getting destroyed and dominated, He will take a step back, point at all of them lying on the ground and say what Smokey said to Deebo in Ice Cube's "Friday" movie: "Damn! You got knocked...tha fuck out!!!"

CHAPTER ONE

<u>Christians are Bear-ly awake</u>

They say it's best to let a sleeping dog sleep or let a sleeping bear sleep. In most cases I can agree with that. But if I'm using the Church as the bear in this book, I'm gonna need the bear to get his ass up.

It has power that no other organization on this planet can match! It has so much strength that it should *never* lose a fight, skirmish, tussle or battle against an inferior and weaker opponent! Ever!

Just like the bear is the most powerful meat-eating animal on the planet, the Church is the most powerful organization on the planet, yet it has no balls and nobody knows exactly what it stands for because it lies down for everything and everyone.

It's time the church woke the fuck up and started acting like a church. It's time the world knew what the church stands for. It's time the *church* knows what it's supposed to be standing for.

I'm so mad at the church I can't stand it! Why am I so mad? I'm so mad because I had been taught all these years that as a Christian, I am supposed to be passive. I am supposed to turn the other cheek if somebody slaps the taste out of my mouth. I'm supposed to be meek, mild and shut the fuck up.

In terms of how humans are supposed to act in the face of injustice, hate and corruption, we have been given images of Martin Luther King, Jr. instead of Malcolm X. We're supposed to be more like Mother Theresa and less like Angela Davis.

They aren't all professing Christians, but they were recognized for taking a stand and creating a dramatic shift in millions of peoples thinking for good causes.

They were influencing and creating a shift in mentality that
Christians should be doing.

We took the advice of the church and marched like Martin
said; while being attacked, beaten up and killed by police, hit with
bricks and spit on by angry mobs and had police dogs biting men,
women and children. We were also peaceful and quiet as lambs
like Theresa. Did that strategy work?

What the church needed was a little more of the "If you hit
me, I will hit you back. If you kill my sons, I will kill your sons. If
you shoot at me, I will shoot at you" mentality of Malcolm and
some of that "I'm black and I'm proud and I'm human and I
deserve to be treated with respect like anybody else" attitude of
Angela.

The Bible says Christians are supposed to be mild, right? And
doesn't it also say Christians are lost sheep in need of a shepherd?

And Christians are supposed to love everybody no matter what they do to us…right???

Not true. As I dug into the Bible and the Lost Books of the Bible, I realized aggression is supposed to be the name of the game for Christians. Being passive is not supposed to be in my vocabulary and it's definitely not in my heavenly bloodline.

Jesus is described as a lion. He is the Lion of Judah. He is also described as a lamb. Even as a lamb, though, He was aggressive and bold in the face of deadly opposition.

He aggressively and intentionally sacrificed Himself. He was the lamb who sacrificed Himself to legally correct the systems of the world and bring them back under the control of humans.

He even let the Governor know, in no uncertain terms, that, "If I wanted to, I could call out to my Father and He would dispatch legions of angels to stop my persecution and death. But I won't. I will let you do what needs to be done because it's part of a bigger plan. My Father's plan. Now, let's get this show on the road..."

I like to describe myself as a lion. A lion takes what he wants when he wants. Sometimes, he doesn't even have to fight. His presence alone, often times by himself, is enough to make most animals in the African safari run away.

Even *Satan* is described as a lion. One of the authors in the Bible writes, "...Satan roams the Earth like a roaring lion, looking to see who he can devour, kill, attack and deceive..."

What is the church described as being? Does the mention of the church strike fear in anybody's hearts? Has anybody said, "Oh shit!! The Christians are coming! The Christians are coming! You better get your shit together because they don't fuck around! They don't tolerate anybody disrespecting their belief system!"

I'll answer that one for you: "NO!" I'll go so far as saying, "Fuck no!" I'll even go a little farther and say, "Hell no! Shit no!

Fuck no! Heck no!" Can you feel what I'm saying? If not, I will gladly repeat myself.

I know some of you holy-rollers, people who say "Oh shoot" instead of "Oh shit" and pure-as-snow Christians who have never done anything wrong in your life are sitting there shaking your heads and praying to *God* I don't repeat all that blasphemy! LOL!!!

Like I said earlier, Christians are given softer labels like meek, humble, loving, tender, non-judgmental, even-tempered, mild-mannered, caring and sweet.

If we were to be given non-human labels to describe us, they would be Charmin toilet tissue, down-filled pillows, feathers, baby chicks, fluffy snow or puppy's fur.

In all fairness to the church, I can say there is an animal that describes how the church and Christians should act and that is a bear. The church is like a group of powerful, sleeping bears.

Bears that are all bundled up and snuggled nice and comfy-like in a quiet cave where no one can disturb their sleep.

Did you know if you are walking near its' hibernating spot, you would never know the bear was there? The only way you would know is if you *literally* stepped right on top of the burrow thing.

That's kind of how Christians are. There are neighborhoods and cities around the world that are living in poverty; while there is a church on every other block with the pastor driving a current-year Mercedes.

There are decisions made in political offices by Christian politicians that are based on greed and how much money they are offered by Big Business...how does that happen? I'll tell you:

Actually, I will tell you how, but not right now. I just remembered that is the topic of the last chapter...

I was studying the life of Jesus and realized how aggressive He was. Even as a young boy, He was known as being aggressive.

Now, those of you who only study the Bible and don't want to hear about anything outside of the Bible, this next part may not be for you...

Me and my wife began to study the Lost Books of the Bible and it helped us understand Jesus and everybody in the Bible on a much deeper, personal level.

Those of you unfamiliar with the Lost Books, let me catch you up. The Bible is made up of 66 separate books by probably 50 different authors (some authors wrote multiple books). This collection of 66 books was made after the committee to write the Bible had gone through thousands of ancient records and manuscripts.

For obvious reasons, you can't carry around a book that basically has a thousand books/stories in it. They narrowed it down to our present-day Bible. The Lost Books are the books that didn't make the cut. Does that mean out of 10,000 manuscripts and records only 66 are historically accurate and true? No. Quick example…

I wrote a short autobiography of my life. My life, just like any of yours, is made up of thousands of events and situations that happened, are real and very true.

If I was to include every, single event in my life, the autobiography would have been an unmanageable 5,000-page book; instead, I chose to narrow it down to around 150 pages.

Does that mean all of the other events and situations in my life aren't true and never happened since they aren't in my book? No. Same concept holds true in my view regarding the Bible.

These lost books tell stories of how aggressive Jesus was as a young child. Oh yeah, if you want to know more about this part of Jesus' life, check out the book, "The Virgin and the Gun." It goes into more detail than I will here. Anyways…

One of the stories say Jesus was a young boy and one of his friends, or just some other boy, accidentally ran into Him. Jesus got mad and told him to die. The boy instantly died. Sounds crazy, huh? I know! I know! But it makes sense.

Jesus was a human little boy. Little boys are aggressive and don't always know how to handle their tempers and physically control themselves when they are mad. Since Jesus was supposed to live life fully as a human, it makes sense that He went through this same process; except when He got mad, He had to learn how to use His supernatural powers properly.

Jesus came to Earth from Heaven and was full of power and confidence. He showed signs of this at an early age and carried this same attitude all the way through His adult life that we know about.

The story about Him killing that boy apparently wasn't a random story. He supposedly had many incidents like that one to the point where His neighbors were constantly complaining to His mom and dad. "His temper is out of control!" and "We don't want this young boy around us with these special powers He uses to kill and hurt our kids" was what a lot of people had to say on record about Him in His early years.

Why did I take so much time out to tell you about Jesus and His aggressive nature as a young child? I did it because He is what the church is based off of. The church is supposed to take on the mentality of its' leader and founder and that person is Jesus.

He was aggressive and bold with everybody from His parents to the top religious leaders of His day. There was a story in both the Bible and the Lost Books that talk about Jesus teaching the religious leaders for 3 days in the temple when He was about 12 years old.

His parents had accidentally left Him behind, so He was just chillin' and schoolin' the groups of adults who came to listen to

Him. When His parents finally caught up with Him, He was like, "When you noticed I wasn't with you, why did you panic? Don't you know I'm exactly where I'm supposed to be? I'm in my Father's house."

That wasn't an apology. That was a bold statement that let His parents know He had business on the floor that needed to be taken care of.

In the book, "Fuck that fig tree!: a Jesus Story", there are many more examples of Jesus being aggressive. These stories involve Jesus approaching a demon-possessed man who He healed. He really didn't have to do too much to heal him.

When the demon realized it was Jesus approaching the man whose body he was possessing, the demon begged Jesus to let him take possession of a nearby pig after He was about to face the inevitable exiting of the man's body.

In this book, I referred to the church as a bear or as a family of bears and that was 100% intentional: Jesus was aggressive as a bear. Not a sleeping bear like His current-day followers; He was a bear who was ready to attack with or without being provoked or poked.

In the stock market, there are two animal references that sum up all of the investor gambling that is done on Wall Street. The Bull and the Bear.

A Bull Market is said to be the aggressive market. A bull is a very aggressive animal and during a market that is considered bullish, the gambling done on the markets favor buyers.

Everybody is aggressive. Everybody is happy. Everybody wants to make a ton of money and they gamble aggressively buying stocks.

A Bear Market is a slower market. Even though the bear is a very aggressive animal, in the minds of stock market gamblers, he represents the slower side of things.

During a Bear Market, the gaming action shifts out of doubt and fear and everybody changes their bets and start selling stocks. Now that I think about it, I should have called the church the Bull instead of the Bear because the Bull represents an aggressive market.

But I'm not going to change now...I already started the book and I am *not* about to rename it because the stock market gamblers chose to call the non-aggressive market a Bear Market.

The analogy of Christians being bears and aggressive still plays itself out with the stock market example. During a Bear Market, there is still a lot of aggressive action. It's just that the aggressiveness stems from fear and doubt.

Once again, the bear *is* depicted as an aggressive animal; but unlike Christians, when they are typically scared or have doubts, they take no aggressive action whatsoever.

I have no idea what the church's stance is on homosexual marriage. I know what the Bible's stance is. I know what God's stance is. It's the *church's* stance that I don't know and as a member of the body of Christ, that's not a good thing.

The name of this book is, "Poke the Bear." As you can maybe see from my examples, even though a bear may not be aggressive until provoked, they are still extremely powerful. Whether or not they have power isn't in question. What *is* in question, as it relates to the church being a bear, is their lack of understanding about what their power is and trying to figure out why they don't use it.

In the end, it would be nice to see the church wake up and take a stand for everything Jesus, its' aggressive leader, stood, and stands for.

Time for tolerating a sleepy-ass church is over.

Time for rolling-over on every issue society deals with is over.

Time for avoiding confrontation as a church body is over.

Time for allowing Satan, evil and corruption to run rampant in society is over, and it's time to end this chapter on how the church is like a sleeping bear.

CHAPTER TWO

<u>Christians *should be* Bear-y mad</u>

Christians in particular should be very mad. Actually, they should be madder than just mad. They should be bear-y mad. That means, "they should be mad as a bear who just go poked."

We all want to be a part of something. You can try and deny it and fight it, but it's true. I'm not saying we all want to join mafias, gangs or book clubs, but we all want to feel loved and needed in some way.

Some of us buy pets. They love us unconditionally. They don't care if we just lost our job or flunked a math test...all they want to do is love us and us, as their owner, love it!

In a quest for love, some of us have joined organizations like political parties. You may be thinking, "Why in the fuck would anybody looking for love join a political party?"

People join them because of the networking, love and control political parties offer. Everybody has their own view love. I don't need to go into the love people had, and have, for Donald Trump. That pollical-party love made some of his supporters perform one of the most disrespectable, treasonable and unpunished acts on American soil we have witnessed since the 9/11 attacks.

There is a sense of pride you get when your party is in control of politics, because it makes you feel like *you* are in control of political decisions somehow...and you, as a voting citizen, love it!

Some people join gangs and mafias for love. There is a sense of power and control knowing there are people who have your back.

Police officers enjoy the Code of the Blue, an unwritten code that allows them to operate above the law; enjoying an untouchable attitude...and they love it!

Gangsters in gangs and mafias join for an array of reasons, the basic of which is belonging. If you grow up in a certain area or are from a certain culture, it can almost be a requirement for survival; while other times it is a matter of just wanting to be a part of something...and they love it!

That leads us to Christians. Most Christians are Christians by what I call default; especially in America. In America for instance, you are either a Christian or a Muslim. That seems to be the 2 most popular choices. I can't really speak on how Islam or being a Muslim works, so I won't.

There is a growing group of people who have said, "fuck religion." They say this because Islam is described as being full of terrorists who just want to blow up innocent people including women and kids; while Christianity is described as being full of hypocrites who tell you to be honest and don't drink or do drugs...as they get drunk, party and cheat on their spouses.

I get it. I get it. I get it. As a Christian, I hate to admit it...but I get it. I grew up in a church where nobody drank, smoked, cheated, cussed or did anything wrong until...until I got older and literally saw these Christians in strip clubs, battling drug and alcohol addictions and doing a bunch of other crazy shit they aren't supposed to be doing.

How do I know? Like I said, I *saw* them. I was right there doing drugs and drinking with some of them. I was at the strip club having a good time with some of them; especially with one of my favorite strippers who used to give me lap dance specials while she "did this until she graduated college."

Knowing how the world views Christians, me included, began to make me very mad! I'm not mad at them or their views. I'm actually mad at us Christians and *our* views! It took me until just a year or so before the writing of this book (January of 2022) for me to change my view, wake up and start acting like a fucking Christian is supposed to.

I was more than mad! I was bear-y mad! I was mad at the fact that I was so much more powerful than I knew I was! I was mad because I was living so far below the level God wanted me to be living! I was mad because I had been going to church my whole life and still didn't know shit about what I was supposed to be doing as a Christian! I was very mad! I mean, I was bear-y mad!

Jesus was constantly getting mad. I think it's important to take a look at what was making Him mad, so that Christians will know exactly who and what to focus their anger on once they get poked. Yup, you already know I put it in a list, a very short list:

1. Religious leaders who don't practice what they preach,

and,

2. Religious leaders who don't preach what they are

supposed to be preaching about

And that about sums up what really mad Him mad. The

majority of times we read about Jesus getting mad can be directly

linked to the religious leaders.

The religious leaders. Jesus was constantly getting mad at

them. He was arguing with them on what seemed like a daily

basis and cussing them out in His own way. He would call them

snakes and vipers and tell them they were actually leading people

away from God and straight to Hell. Why was He saying these

things and getting angry with them?

During His 1st sermon, He warned the people that they

needed to step their game up as it related to getting knowledge about true spiritual matters. He then let it be known that the

current leaders of the law and religion didn't know shit.

To emphasis this point, He said, "If you want to get to

Heaven, you can forget about it unless…unless you know more

about the scriptures than they do." He didn't exactly say He was

mad at them in this example, but He was putting them on notice

that He didn't think very highly of them.

I began to get mad at everything churchy. My wife had

told me about a revival she wanted to attend. She was super

excited because the guest host/announcer/hype man was a

person she loved to listen to. In fact, he was the reason why she

liked revivals in the 1st place.

I decided to go because we operate as a family. I knew I

would hate it and I did. I told her upfront exactly what he was

going to say and he said it!

He was like a lot of people who misused their titles. Just because he was able to get loud and get people excited, he relished the title he had that put him on stage that night. I am not singling him out because I have gone to a couple of revivals and they all had the same result.

In this case, after he had worked the small crowd into a frenzy of sweaty, dancing and loud-pray excited children waiting for his promise to give them some candy, he dropped the bomb. It went something like this:

"Ladies and gentlemen! I have a word from God today for you! God told me to tell each and every one of you to come up front and put $500 in the collection plate! Now, I know $500 may seem like a lot, but it's not! I know some of you spend that much in weave and makeup...in month. All I'm doing is reminding you that this is not from me, but it is directly from God and I am here to deliver this message to you so you can be saved! You give that $500 and God will bless you for listening to His personal request."

After this 1st unsuccessful round of accumulating funds had passed, he adjusted his pitch, and it went something like this:

"Ladies and Gentlemen! I have another word from God for you today! He knows $500 may be a lot for some of you to bear, so He was using that as a test to see who of you was able to pass the test. $250!!! $250 is the next number God has placed in my head. He wants to make sure you aren't going to miss out on the blessings He has in store for you this week just because you aren't able to give $500. Isn't God a good God????

Well, what the MC of the hour didn't know, because apparently God had forgot to tell him, was that the people in this church didn't have that kind of money to drop in the plate. Soooooo, after another unsuccessful round of raising capital "for God," he was apparently inspired and allowed to adapt his pledge amount to accommodate his target audience. The next round of funding sounded like this:

"Ladies and Gentlemen! I know how hard it is to come up with $500 or even $250. And if I know it, you have to believe my God, *our* God, knows it. In light of this new understanding, God has asked me to open this round of raising capital, I mean, *raising money for the uplifting of His word,* and request that anybody who has any amount of money to give to God, to come forward and do so.

The funny part about all this shit was that he eventually opened the offering to people who had $20 or less!! LOL LOL LOL!! I was like, "What in the fuck did I just witness???"

My wife was extremely disappointed. Here was this man who she respected as a pastor and an excellent revival leader, a man of God…and I was able to tell her *exactly* what he was going to do step-by-step without ever having heard of him before.

Before I get back into why Jesus was leery about people with religious titles, I did go to a revival a couple years ago.

During this revival, the minister had everyone worked up again and right before he asked for some crowd-funding money "for God," he ceremoniously fell out on the floor.

When he started to hit the floor, his chosen elders and the church "nurse" who was on standby for this event, rushed to his aid, making his fall as graceful and elegant as possible. I had to admit, it was smoothly done. Staged…but not staged. Definitely professional.

I was in the front row watching it all…without offering assistance. I didn't have to because I knew his team of highly decorated staff around him, with their badges, gloves and special uniforms for revivals would tend to him.

Upon "waking up," he immediately explained to his loyal flock what the reason was for the sudden fall: God had a word for him. It was a word, "…so powerful that it knocked me off my feet."

This crowd must have had access to more funding and apparently God was aware of this stroke of good luck and passed it on to His messenger. The 1st round of funding at the other revival I told you about was $500...not this one! He started at $5,000 and worked his way down to $100.

After he had people come up front with their $100 pledge, he told everybody who wasn't able to give $100 to hold their hands high in the air with whatever it was they could afford and then he prayed over it. He wanted to pray over it to make sure that, even though these monetary pledges to God didn't meet the minimum financial requirements God had in mind, he still wanted them and their pledge to be blessed.

Alright, enough of that. My point is to tell you that people like this really began to get me mad! I was mad that they were misusing their title for personal gain. There is no way God is going to work like that!

What also made me mad is that the church has gotten accustomed to this kind of practice. There is a pastor named Benny Hinn. He is on the big screen and is raking in millions of dollars.

Part of his thing is to wield the power of his church title over the masses and heal them. Somehow, his position as pastor has given him a direct line to God the rest of us don't have and has allowed him to heal any disease with a quick donation to the "general fund" and a touch of his all-powerful, all-healing hand on just the right spot.

He is not alone. I used to love Joel Osteen. He gave messages that were as sunny as the day was long. I felt good when I would always see his smiling face. I knew he would start off with a nice joke that would end with him flashing his perfect set of teeth on the screen as he laughed at his own joke.

Once I began to *really* listen to his message, I began to get bear-y mad! He is preaching a sunny-side up message to millions of people and making millions of dollars preaching a message that isn't even close to the message Jesus told the religious leaders they should be preaching.

Jesus said from His 1st sermon that He came to preach the message about the Kingdom. He wasn't interested in telling people that every day would be sunny. Through His parable-lessons He revealed more of a, what people would call "doomsday" message.

He was telling people that they needed to understand this Kingdom stuff; because if they didn't, they would pretty much burn in hell. He was constantly saying this is the only message that needs to be preached.

He even linked the message about the Kingdom to the end of the world as we know it. Everybody seems to know when the end of the world will come. Oh, I have to tell you a quick story...

I was living in Detroit working on roof on the Westside. I was presented with an offer to do a quick insurance job on a new vehicle. I was going to take the job until I remembered it was almost New Years of 2000.

According to every news channel, historian and astrologer on the planet, the world was *definitely* going to end at exactly 1 second after midnight. I declined the job because I drank the koolaid and believed the world would end or at least start ending in 2000 like the experts said and I did *not* want to be stuck in a jail cell if shit went bad while the world was ending.

Well, the next day the world was still going around the Sun so I decided to take the job. I was in jail by 3pm the next day!

The end-of-times message was able to postpone me going to jail for a day, so I suppose it had its' purpose. Continuing on...

What reminded me of that story? I was reminded of it because Jesus said, "Don't worry about all the end-of-time signs you will see such as war and famine. They all have to happen as part of the process. **The end will not come until THIS message has been preached around the whole world."**

The end of the world isn't coming until the message of the Kingdom has been preached everywhere. So, based on my understanding and calculations about the messages the pulpit has been delivering, we have another 200 years or so. Preachers haven't been focused on the Kingdom message and probably won't be inclined to do so in the very near future.

Did that make me mad? Yes! It made me mad because Jesus is giving the church instructions and lessons left and right and its' religious leaders aren't paying attention.

Joel Osteen is a religious leader who hasn't spoken a word about homosexual marriage, addiction, cheating husbands and wives or any important subject that society deals with. If he can't speak on those issues, I *know* he isn't about to change his format and talk about the consequences of not understanding the Kingdom message.

If he did that, it would cut off his tithe funding. While I'm talking about him, Jesus said he was sick and tired of the religious leaders like Joel for not practicing what they preached. Everyone with a phone and internet know it was Joel Osteen who could have used his multi-million-dollar church facility to help thousands of people during the hurricane.

If you'll notice, I said "could have." I said that because even though as a pastor he is supposed to be teaching people to help others, etc. he decided to NOT let people have access to his newly-renovated church building during a national disaster that was on his doorstep. Literally!

Let me not talk about our religious leaders and double-back to talk about why Jesus was disgusted with them and was bear-y mad at them 99% of the time.

One day He had healed a man who was paralyzed by telling Him, "Don't worry. Your sins are forgiven." The religious leaders who were present started thinking in their heads that Jesus was blaspheming. They were saying He was disrespecting God because they didn't think He had the ability to forgive sins.

Jesus knew what they were thinking and put them in their place. He said, "Look, I know what you're thinking, so how about this. I do have the legal power to forgive sins; but if you don't like the way I said it, I can also do it in a way that your simple ass can understand. Would it be better if I just told him to pick up his mat and walk? If so, it doesn't matter to me. I can do it either way." And with that statement, Jesus healed the man by saying, "Pick up your mat and walk."

That seems to be a common theme in His day and today with religious leaders. Once someone gets the title of pastor of "leader of the flock" or "pope" or has 3 degrees in the study of all things Biblical, they tend to think they are experts. I agree they are experts, but they often take their knowledge to an unnecessary and borderline, sac-religious level.

By that I mean people with high religious titles tend to be stuck in their ways. They think they deserve to be held in high respect and that their views are always right. If you don't believe me, try talking to your pastor and suggesting there is a different way to look at a subject found in the Bible.

He will most likely tell you that your view is "interesting" but that you need to go back and check your Bible studies a little deeper before you try and have a Bible-battle with someone on his level.

And PLEASE make sure you don't test my theory on someone with multiple titles! Sweet Jesus!! Going up against a person who is not only a deacon or pastor but also has the title of "high priest of the holy order of the divine masters of the virgin Mary" or some other lengthy title will surely put an "L" on your religious score record!

Why am I irritated with people who walk around with fancy titles? Because Jesus was mad about it. He said they were more focused on what their titles were than on actually preaching and teaching what they were supposed to.

He said, "Some of you want to be called 'teacher' but you're not teachers...there is only one who should be called 'teacher' and that is the Messiah."

Speaking about titles, Jesus asked His disciples what people were calling Him. The responses He got were, John the

Baptist or that He was one of the great prophets from the past who is now reborn; such as Jeremiah or Elijah.

I think most pastors would be proud to be thought of as a great prophet of God who was brought back to life. Not Jesus. When the disciple Peter said, "I think you are the Messiah. The Son of the Living God," Jesus was happy.

That is the only "title" He needed to hear. In fact, He never went around and told people to call Him 'Pastor Jesus' or 'High Reverend to the High Priest Jesus.'

The religious leaders tried to trip Jesus up and asked Him to give them a sign from Heaven. They wanted Him to do something that proved He was truly divine like He said.

He got irritated with them and told them only wicked people ask for a sign and then walked off. Once I saw how irritated Jesus was about this topic, I got irritated about it.

I didn't know it until I heard one of my favorite gospel songs that had these lyrics in it: We are waiting on you, Jesus! We are expecting a miracle from you! We are expecting signs from you! We are expecting you to do miracles in our lives right now, Jesus!

I used to love that song until I paid attention to the lyrics. When she sings about wanting a sign and miracles from Jesus, I was like, "Is she just singing something to get people hyped and excited, or is she actually singing about things Jesus said He would do for us?"

At that point, I began to pay closer attention to the songs I was listening to. I no longer wanted to just sing songs that "give praise to God" that directly contradict what Jesus is telling us to expect. That type of stuff began to make me bear-y mad!

We are supposed to sing praises to God as part of our worship. Now I began to look at a lot of gospel artists and question their motivation. Were they just interested in singing songs that got people out their seats and on an emotional high that was based on wrong expectations?

In the end, I decided to show compassion to the musical artists. They were simply leading people in praise based on the messages they were accustomed to listening to. I stopped being mad at them. I had to realize that my eyes had just been opened and I needed people to have compassion on me to get me to this point.

I didn't stop being mad at the religious leaders! These are the ones that flaunt their religious degrees and titles in our faces; while they aren't living the way they are supposed to be.

Should I show them compassion? Yes. But at this stage in the game, I'm not ready to. I'm still bear-y mad with them and unsure how I am supposed to proceed with my view on religious leaders and the church.

For now, I have decided to work on myself and as I learn about the Kingdom Message, I will share it with as many people I can as I go throughout my days with my books as well as by my actions.

CHAPTER THREE

Christians need to get their Bear-ings

A bearing is something that has to do with direction. I'm quite sure ship captains and explorers use bearings, or bearing lines, to get from Point A to Point B.

As you can probably tell, I am not as familiar with bearings as I probably should be, but I know enough about the concept bearings represent. They represent something significant: direction. Without direction, you will never get to the final destination of your choosing.

Christians don't seem to have bearings or a sense of bearing. They don't know which way to go or which way they should be going. In my view, they don't know what a church really is *or* what Jesus wants from the church. That's not good.

How do I know? Because I'm a Christian and I have no clue what the church is doing or what it stands for. The only things I know about the Christian church from fairly recent history are from American slavery and politics and also the Crusades.

Christianity was used to make American slavery morally correct; while American politics, based on "In God we Trust," routinely is involved in so much scandalous, corrupt, greedy and treasonous actions against the American people that it's ridiculous.

Where does that leave Christians direction-wise? Absolutely nowhere and somewhere at the same time. Let me stop using metaphors and just get straight into what I'm trying to say about Christianity…

The term Christian represents the leader and founder of the church. Over the years and many language translations, He has become known as Jesus Christ. Followers of Jesus Christ were then said to follow the religion called Christianity. The entire

church system and basis of Christianity is supposed to be Christ-

centered.

Here's the thing. Our modern church hasn't been paying

attention to what the fuck they were supposed to be doing form

the beginning! Jesus tells us that He was setting up His church

based on two facts. These are, 1) He was indeed the Messiah and

2) He was indeed the Son of God.

Before we talk about the significance of being both the

Messiah and the Son of God, we have to talk about what He

wanted His church to look like. We got the term church from a

Greek term, the final language to translate most of the scriptures,

ecclesia.

The ecclesia was a body of citizens who all had voting

power. They voted on any legislation that would have an effect

on their personal, social and financial lives. They had influence.

They had power. They had citizenship. They voted because

voting was used to carry out its' most, purest form:

representation. The citizens had their rights protected and

represented through voting.

So, when Jesus said He was building a church body, He was

referring to the building up of citizens who would come together

as one and have power and influence in society. In order to

understand what areas His church was supposed to wield

influence in, you would 1st have to look at the 2 points I

mentioned earlier. Let's take a look now...

The Messiah. Jesus said He was building His church on the

grounds of Him being the Messiah. The Messiah is a King or High

Priest. He is someone who is anointed by God for a specific

purpose. In the eyes of the Israelites and Jewish people, the

Messiah was going to be the one to help their culture rise to

political and financial power and dominance in the world.

Jesus was very particular about who He gave His Kingdom message to. In one instance, a non-Jewish woman asked Jesus to teach her some things and He said, "No. The message of the Kingdom is not for dogs." He would eventually, after seeing her faith in Him, give in and bless her because of her persistence and faith in Him.

After Jesus died and rose again, He then instructed His disciples in what has become known as the Great Commission, to, "Go and make disciples of all nations; baptizing them in the name of the Father, the Son and the Holy Spirit."

Without getting into too much technical theology or church stuff, Jesus was basically saying He wanted all the nations of the world to become students/disciples of His teachings. And THAT is the direction the church is supposed to be taking!

Seems simple enough, but it's not. The church I know has been content with typically sending white missionaries to black and brown-skinned nations to help build schools and churches and pass out medicine. That is not what Jesus was talking about directly.

The reason for going to all the nations was to teach the Kingdom message. That is the primary message He was concerned with. It's cool to go help "uncivilized" people come to understand who White Jesus is and to let them know that the missionaries are there to help them and that they come from a white-God-fearing country built on Bible principals...but that's not what Jesus wanted.

Kingdom message. He talked about it in His 1st sermon and pretty much all of His parables. When He sent out His 12 disciples, He instructed them to, "...proclaim THIS message: the Kingdom of Heaven has come near."

Instead of the church trying to look like Good Samaritans and spending millions of dollars to have some type of presence and influence all around the world under the name of Christianity, it should have been focused on teaching the people they reached about the Kingdom. They should have been teaching people how to help themselves and become independent.

I have to tell you what the Kingdom Message is in my view. The Kingdom Message is the teaching about the Kingdom. It is a message that teaches people the power they have as citizens of an actual kingdom called Heaven.

It is a message that lets people know there is a higher power and authority that runs the natural order of things and if you have just the slightest bit of faith in that system, you will achieve dual citizenship. You will be citizens of Heaven *and* whatever country you live in.

Becoming a citizen under a King means that King *has* to take care of you. You are one of his citizens, and if the world sees a kingdom full of lazy, greedy, hypocritical citizens, that will look bad on the King himself. It is in the king's best interest to do whatever He can to lift the status and lifestyles of his citizens.

When Jesus came and legally took control of the world systems, taking the power away from Satan back into the hands of humans, our heavenly Father gave Him "all authority in Heaven and on Earth."

Do you remember a parable about the bags of gold? It's the one where a rich man left to go to another country to become king. Before he goes, he leaves some of his wealth to 3 servants. They are given wealth based on how good they have proven themselves in the past with it.

When the man returned, as a king, he called the 3 servants and they showed him what they did with the wealth he trusted each of them with. The ones who took their wealth and made a profit were rewarded. The king said he would put them in charge of many things.

The last servant didn't invest the wealth at all. The king did 2 things. He 1st took away the wealth that servant had and gave it to the person who started off with the highest amount of wealth and then took that servant's position away from him; calling him worthless, evil and lazy.

The meaning of that parable is this: Jesus was the rich man who left to become king. As we know, after He died and rose from the grave, a short time later He was witnessed as having left Earth and went back to Heaven. God has given Him all authority in Heaven and Earth. He had officially become King. He left here to get His new title.

The wealth represented Kingdom Knowledge. Whoever has shown the capacity to retain and apply the principles Jesus was constantly teaching would receive as much information as they could take in.

The more you are able to show Jesus that you not only can retain Kingdom Knowledge, but you can also apply it properly and get results, He can trust you and put you in positions of power and influence. He will "put you in charge of many things."

The lessons learned in that parable sum of the entire direction and purpose of the church. Like I said, it's always a good thing when you go somewhere and help people; but if you truly are a church that wants to send people out in the direction Jesus wanted and wants His church to go, then you need to send your missionaries out strapped with as much Kingdom Knowledge as they have proven they can handle AND apply.

Remember Jesus said He was basing His church on the fact that He was in fact the Messiah or King? Well, it takes faith to believe He came from a kingdom called Heaven, was born an infant human on Earth, died and then rose from the dead, returned to Heaven to take His rightful place in the Kingdom next to His Father and has the ability to do everything He said He can and will do.

In order to be a Kingdom citizen, you have to believe He is King. You have to believe and understand He has all authority on Heaven and Earth. Once you have that mindset, you will live differently and you will know what direction you are supposed to take.

Getting your bearings is all about directions. Jesus clearly says that collectively as a church body, we are supposed to be focused on the Kingdom Message; because that leads to living a certain lifestyle. That hasn't happened in the church because the church isn't aware that it's supposed to be heading in the Kingdom Message direction.

The Crusades are about the earliest recoded events in

Christian history that are significant. During these basically

military operations, the church went around killing, robbing and

stealing shit "in the name of God and the church." How that fits

in with the Kingdom Message I have no ideal.

Jesus came to fulfill the law. Those aren't my words.

Those are His. He came to take care of legal matters...not

religious. A kingdom is all about the law, and He fulfilled the

requirement of the law with His blood to legally take up His

position as king.

In the introduction, I mentioned something about how

powerful a bear is when I referenced the church as a bear. Can

you see where I was going with that? Are you getting your

bearings? Are you getting a sense of what way you are supposed

to be going and how you are supposed to act?

The creator of the universe is your Heavenly Father. You know Him on a 1st name, personal basis. He is family. He has a son who left one kingdom to establish another one. His entire goal was to put you and I in royal positions. He wanted us to legally be able to have access to both Heaven and worldly assets.

We are legally royalty! Our legal inheritance is found in both Heaven AND this life! Our goal, contrary to what the church preaches, is NOT to suffer in this life so we can get to Heaven.

God made Earth for us. This is our kingdom. We legally gave it over to Satan and Jesus legally got it back for us. That is the position we are to be acting from.

Jesus acknowledged Satan was prince of this world without hesitation. As we learned from the Parable of the Bags of Gold though, Jesus had to die and rise from the dead and "go to a faraway country to be crowned king."

He is the King of Kings. We are Kings and Queens on this Earth. We are the rightful rulers and we are supposed to instill law and order based on God's laws. That means we are supposed to act upon all the laws and guidance Jesus laid out before us. As citizens of the Kingdom of Heaven, we are supposed to set up churches.

The church/ecclesia is supposed to be how we dominate the world systems. Christians who have their bearings, or have their shit together, are supposed to act like this:

1. We are supposed to be in all the top positions of every industry on this planet to make sure it runs according to God's laws.

2. When we see corruption in politics and Big Business, we are supposed to step in and make whatever changes are necessary to correct it.

3. Widows and orphans are supposed to be a top priority according to God.

4. We are supposed to pray in private.

5. We are supposed to fast.

6. We are supposed to treat people how we want to be

    treated.

7. We are supposed to control animal and plant populations

    wisely.

8. We are supposed to manage Earth's resources in a

    responsible manner.

9. We are supposed to give to the needy in private.

10. We are supposed to fight anything and everyone who

    goes against God's laws.

THAT is the direction the church is supposed to be heading

in. those are some of the examples Jesus taught in His messages

about life on Earth. We are supposed to be like brand

ambassadors for Heaven.

I watched a video that this young boy did. He was the heir to

some big pharmaceutical company. Him and a lot of his friends felt bad and uncomfortable because they were inheriting millions of dollars without having to work for it.

Some of his friends were extremely cocky, conceited and felt like they were the most powerful people on the planet. Why? Because of their inheritance. Somebody had done all the work so they could enjoy life with an inheritance that amounted to large sums of material wealth.

They felt like their wealth gave them power. Some of them had the confidence to become super models; while others had the boldness to say they could buy anybody they wanted.

Jesus did what He legally did so that we could have an inheritance also. Our inheritance is in both Heaven and on Earth. We are supposed to be as bold, if not bolder, than the kids in that documentary.

We have more than just material wealth. We have access to

all the resources in Heaven as well as whatever it is we need on

Earth to wield our God-given power in the world systems.

Jesus said, "Based on the knowledge and facts that I am the

Messiah, the Son of the Living God, I will build my church." The

direction of the church should be clear from that one, simple-yet-

powerful statement:

Operate from a position of royal power and authority to

influence the entire world based on God's laws.

<u>SUMMARY</u>

In the end, I may be too hard on the church, almost to the point of distaste for it. If so, I don't apologize. I used to literally cry in guilt and shame when I realized how much my heavenly Father put into this thing called life and how much Jesus sacrificed to help put it all back together...for me.

I was like the Prodigal Son. I was royalty but preferred to wallow in the mud with pigs and run through the gutters with the roaches and the rats getting high. Once I got over my pity party, I started to get my bearings.

I was bear-y mad at how I had allowed myself to remain under the control of Satan and sin for so long; when all along, Jesus had legally put me in the position where I was to dominate Satan and

sin.

My anger helped me get my bearings and I will continue to

poke the bear until the entire church body wakes its' ass up and

starts acting like a powerful, Kodiak grizzly who just got poked and

woken up early out of hibernation! A bear who is ravenously

ready to make up for lost time!

BONUS ESSAYS:

In the back of each book in the "Your View Matters" series is a

section called Private Matters. This section has Bonus Essays.

These essays cover topics that people typically share in private

that I think should be openly shared. Your view on any given topic

matters and so do you. Check out the Bonus Essays in this book:

JESUS FREAK

There is a term thrown around called "Jesus Freak". It was designed to be a put-down on anybody who was seriously into Jesus. It worked. Well, it worked for a little while. I have to admit, it even worked on me...at first.

Following the Bible and being a Christian has always been a social and religious target for people who want to live life on their own terms. Nobody ever attacks Islam, Buddhism, Darwinism but if you mention you are a Christian or if you mention the name "Jesus", here come the sighs and the "why do you always have to talk about Jesus?" reactions.

Here's why. You know what? I was going to do it in paragraph form, but I just changed my mind. I like list's so I'm going to number some of the reasons why:

1. Jesus is the only human who ever claimed to know God
   directly and He had plenty of supporting evidence with His
   actions.

2. Jesus is the only human ever whose death was
   documented and witnessed by many people...and His
   resurrection was also witnessed and documented by many
   people.

3. Jesus is the only human that had documented records
   where He was able to tell storms to die down and to
   control nature.

4. Jesus is the only human who delivered a message that
   talked about getting personal with the creator of the
   Universe. All other religious and spiritual paths talk about
   some "thing" that is not designed for humans to get
   personal with (Islam being an exception...kind of).

5. Jesus is the only human who is recorded as performing
   actual miracles. Miracles that included raising people from
   the dead.

6. Jesus is the only human who gave us a clear explanation for human's purpose on Earth AND tied it into our spiritual origins. All other spiritual walks just tell us to do what we think is right and love everybody and we're gonna be A-ok.

7. Jesus is the only human who has recorded and documented manuscripts written thousands of years before His birth that predicted His coming.

I could go on for ever with this list, but I won't. I think you get the point that Jesus was and is an extraordinary individual. He spent His adult life here on Earth looking out for us. His laser-focus was to let us know that God is real, Satan and sin are real and that since He is the only one who actually witnessed Earth's beginnings and the rise and fall of Satan and sin, His goal was to teach us how to duplicate the Kingdom of Heaven here on Earth.

He also had a ton of lessons about life that, if followed properly, will make any individual find peace, happiness and success in every situation in life. He tied right, wrong, good, bad,

God, Heaven, financial and spiritual wealth together in a way that no one before Him or since Him has been able to do.

If somebody wants to label me as a "Jesus Freak", I gladly accept that title. Actually, you can call me whatever the fuck you want to and I won't be offended or mad. In the case of the "Jesus Freak" label, I will actually shake your hand and thank you. That's a label I will gladly wear.

I have to say something about the "Jesus Freak" thing. A lot of people are finding it fashionable to wear bracelets that say "what would Jesus do" and people like to make social media posts that say "I love Jesus and He is My Lord and Savior. If you agree, please share." And now you got 3,000 mutha fuckas agreeing...but are they actually living like Jesus wants them to?

Do you remember the Lord's prayer? A lot of Believers say that prayer daily or at least a lot. How many of them understand that our purpose on Earth is to create Heaven on Earth? In that prayer, Jesus taught us to ask for "…may your Kingdom come…" That means we are asking for the Kingdom of Heaven to be established on Earth.

How does God work on Earth? Since He gave humans dominion, He rarely just comes in and does whatever He wants to do. He respects His own laws. What God looks for is for humans that He can work through.

The entire Bible if full of recorded events where God has Moses free the slaves, Joshua leading battles and prophets to give messages to world leaders and specific groups of people.

Jesus constantly told people who were interested in His lessons that they had to take action. Believers are supposed to suit up for spiritual warfare. Believers are supposed to stand up against laws that go directly against God's laws such as the legalization of homosexual marriage, corrupt and prejudicial drug sentencing laws and a host of other activity that certain members of society try and legalize so they can try and operate above God's laws.

A real "Jesus Freak" is ready to stand up when the rest of society is bowing down to social pressure. A "Jesus Freak" is an individual who doesn't just wear a *Jesus t-shirt* while he or she is actively involved in activities that destroy our temple such as drinking, vaping and letting their bodies get completely out of shape.

I will close with this: "Jesus Freaks" are the true leaders of society. Don't try and wear this badge without putting in the time. Being a "Jesus Freak" is not designed to be a fad. It involves daily prayer, meditation and conversations with our Heavenly Father, with Jesus and with the Holy Spirit. The key word is "daily". A true "Jesus Freak" does not go to church one hour a week and think that their "God time" quota for the week is satisfied. You don't get to wear the "Jesus Freak" label if that's the only time you tryin' to put in.

"Jesus Freaks", it's time to run shit!!! It's time to stop being scared to stand up for shit!!! It's time to stop letting human governments that contradict Heaven's government to continue to fuck shit up!!! It's time to re-claim your lost shit!!! It's time to start a local Bible Fight Club!!! It's time to do whatever your "Jesus shirts" are telling the world that you do!!!

LET'S DO THIS SHIT FOR REAL, JESUS FREAKS!!!

I'll see the rest of you freaks at the finish line!!!

Christian Trinity…Christian Tragedy

The Church tells Believers that a personal relationship with God and Jesus is the ultimate goal. That's fine and all, but you can't say that and then not explain to us who God is because you think it's a tricky subject.

I've asked several people from pastors to old-timer Believers to please describe who God is. The best answer I've gotten is that He is a personality and so is Jesus and so is the Holy Spirit.

So, let me get this straight: my goal is to get personal with a personality that is somehow made up of 3 personalities? Not gonna happen. Impossible.

I don't know why the religious leaders avoid this subject so much. The more they ignore this important topic, the more I see why Jesus despised the religious leaders of His day. He was always getting into it with them and calling them snakes.

How about this: God is our Father and He is a Being. We are made in His image and He walks and talks and has arms and legs like us. He is NOT Jesus and when Jesus came to Earth, He was NOT God in an earthly body.

The Holy Spirit, God and Jesus are 3 separate Beings. Once I looked at like that, I was finally able to get personal with all 3 in our own way. And I have to admit it felt *extremely* good and my walk with them finally became a reality! I was able to tap into the Father-Son relationship with God by following the example Jesus gave us.

He was always talking about doing what His dad told Him to because He loves His dad and His dad loves Him. Viewing God as a 3-Being, shape-shifter will never get you to the point where you can get personal with Him because you can't get personal with a cloud.

The image of the holy trinity has helped Satan because it keeps us from getting a personal relationship with God. Jesus told us to pray to our Father who is in Heaven. That clearly means Him and God aren't the same Being. He also said, you can talk about me but anybody that talks about the Holy Spirit has committed the only sin that is unforgivable.

Moses was bold and asked God if he could see Him. God said that would be impossible because His glory is too bright. But He did tell Moses He would WALK past him and cover Moses up WITH HIS HANDS so he wouldn't try and look at God's face. God then said, I will uncover you so you can see my BACK as I WALK on to wherever He was headed.

There it is. God has a body, arms, back, legs and a face. Please get personal with Him on a one-on-one basis and stop believing the trinity teaching that God is a 3-Being personality or a mysterious, impersonal "thing" that is made up of 3 other "things." Who's your daddy? God is!

ONE NATION UNDER WHO?? GOD??

The United States government is *designed* and fully capable to distribute justice in its purest form at home and abroad. Our government has established itself as a military and financial powerhouse; but our political process is so full of corruption that it renders any thoughts of effectiveness null and void.

Our Constitution and legal tender both state that we are a God-fearing nation. In light of the fact that we define the protecting of our individual freedoms and rights as the enforcement of a separation between Church and State, can we truly be a God-fearing nation? The resulting, disturbingly high, level of inefficiency and corruption is the natural order of things. A government that claims to be fundamentally based on God-fearing principles and ethics while its hands are tied in regards to incorporating Biblical principles in its rulings is in essence a non-government.

The introduction of the "separation of Church and State" in our Constitution has become a declaration of this country's pious attitude towards God and religion. As noble as it appears to be, that one clause has proven to be the "writing on the wall" for America and has become the gateway clause to allow immoral actions and policies by our governing bodies to be legally enforced without penalty under the law.

I do believe that this country's founding fathers had the right idea by creating a constitution that by that time period's standards appeared to be morally correct. Including the reference to God gave it supernatural power, making it an instant gold-standard document. The Constitution now became a document that could be looked at as "being inspired by God." That reference was intended to be the undefined, moral DNA for all following pieces of legislation.

If America is to be truly great, it must shed its cloak of perceived morality. All evidence of it must be removed from our legislation with the same vigor we pursue terrorists, or human rights violators or those who interfere with the economic interests of lobbyists.

One option is to just call it what it is and ban any reference to God on anything or any process that is government related; at least that way we as citizens know exactly what to expect and we can act accordingly. That is what the current option of doing business in America is: pay who you need to pay in the government to make morally corrupt business/political policies legal...and you are free to make as much money as you want and legally terrorize other American citizens who you don't like based on personal and societal prejudices.

For instance, the government systematically inserted cocaine and automatic weapons into certain areas in society starting in the early 60's, and routinely participates in the sale of both drugs and weapons…then enforces cruel and unusual punishments on the citizens of those same areas that either sell or are caught in the web of drug use and addiction. There are laws that state that if you get caught with possession or in the act of selling $1,000 worth of crack cocaine there are mandatory prison sentences that range from 1 to 5 years in prison; meanwhile, corporations are allowed to (and encouraged to) sell highly addictive "legal pharmaceutical" drugs with horrible side effects, get them approved by paying government agencies/agents and legally engage in price-gouging tactics…all with absolute impunity.

There are cases in the world of finance that are absolutely and immorally wrong; but since the law says "immoral doesn't necessarily constitute illegal"…these billion-dollar companies are allowed to operate outside the law with no fear of legal repercussions.

That's the case with the most recent real-estate market meltdown several years ago. Millions of Americans lost their homes because of predatory lending practices and schemes by

large financial companies who made billions...no one was ever

convicted or sent to prison because "technically" it was all legal.

In fact, after the market collapsed and several billion-dollar

corporations who, after making billions in profits from all the

scheming, began to lose money, they successfully pleaded their

case to the government and asked that they be given multi-

billion-dollar loans to "start over, cover their losses and continue

business as usual".

There is another option that we as a country could take.

We could keep the references to God and actually apply Biblical

principles to our legislation. Unlike the first option, this option

would require more than just the stroke of a pen. This option will

require action. That's the price for taking a stand. The good news

is that America has a long, standing tradition of taking a stand.

This should make the implementation of this option easy. All we

would have to do is change our view on where we stand to where

God stands. This means we no longer take sides with a cultural group or a political party. We now can live up to our name "United States of America" and unite as one body for the good of all people.

We can begin to implement the second option immediately. It's quite easy: Love and respect God *and* love and respect others by treating them how you want to be treated. It's okay if you don't understand the first half of that premise; simply start applying the second half of it and the first half will become second nature. You don't need to call your State Representative to do that or get 1,000 signatures on a petition. Simply treat the next person you see, whether it's your child, your neighbor or your local cashier at your favorite fast-food restaurant, how you would want that person to act towards you or talk to you. That one act will do more for this country right here right now, than any petition or waiting on Congress to get a vote together.

We get mad at the government without realizing that we *are* the government. The government is made up of people. No people. No government. Armed with that power, change has to start on the individual level. Change your view and you change your destiny and the destiny of this country. We as individuals are this country. As our individual views and actions shift towards the good of all people, the views and courses of actions of our country will seamlessly and naturally shift towards the good of all people as well.

God bless America so that we can truly act as one nation under Him like our founding fathers so eloquently stated and strove for in the words of our Constitution.

I, Larry A. Yff, part of "we the people of the United States", in order to form a more perfect Union, establish Justice, insure domestic tranquility, provide for the common defense, promote the general welfare and secure the Blessings of Liberty to

ourselves and our posterity do ordain, establish and approve of

this Constitution in its purest, God-respecting form for the benefit

of the United States of America.

CLASH OF THE CULTURES: CUSS/SLANG WORDS

In any relationship, communication seems to be the bonding agent. Couples therapy involves seeking ways to communicate better. Corporations constantly look for the best ways to communicate and reach their target audience. Different cultures communicate within their culture one way and with other cultural groups another way. To be effective in our personal, business and cross-cultural communications, I believe a better understanding of cuss and slang words needs to be discussed.

Purpose of cuss/slang words:

1. In general, these words are words to convey a high level of emotion or passion. It gives your mind a break from all the formality of our language and lets you enter a more creative frame of mind because some things can't always

be put into words. Example: You are driving down the highway and a car, not just any car, a new model Lamborghini races by doin' no less than 130mph. If I'm telling you about it and I say "I was driving on the Lodge Freeway heading downtown and I was doing about 90mph; when all of a sudden I hear this loud ass roaring sound and this bright red Lamborghini or some shit blows by like I'm fuckin' standin' still! He had to be doing at least 160 fuckin miles an hour! That shit was crazy!" What should that tell you about my character if anything? What was my excitement/passion level and how could you tell? What does my choice of words say about my education level? What does my choice of words say about my spirituality?

- You can't really tell much about me as a person by my response. You can't say I'm a bad dad or a good one; that I'm rich or poor.

- You can tell my excitement level was off the charts.

- You can't tell whether or not I graduated high school or if I have a Master's Degree in International Finance.

- You can't even tell if I'm a Christian or not. If someone can show me in the Bible where it says "the use of a particular word to describe the indescribable is a sin"......

2. Cuss/slang words allow the user to give others warnings as to where they are at emotionally. Example: Somebody keeps calling your phone or sending you text and is annoying you. I text back "Leave me the fuck alone!" What should that tell you about my character if anything? What was my excitement/passion level and how could you tell? What does my choice of words say about my

education level? What does my choice of words say

about my spirituality?

- You can't tell much about my character by

  my response. You can't say I'm a good dad

  or a bad one; that I'm rich or poor.

- You can tell my emotions are running hot

  and on a high level.

- You can't tell my education level by my

  response.

- You can't even tell if I am a Christian or not.

  There is nowhere in the Bible that says you

  have to only use certain words to describe

  your mood when you're angry. It does say

  "don't do anything in anger" and I believe

  that refers to actual actions or regarding

  the use of language you shouldn't say

  something in anger that you will regret. To

me, letting you know that I've had enough and giving you a verbal warning is fair.

3. Believe it or not, cuss/slang words can be a "term of endearment". What is better for a boss to say to a good employee: "Daryl, I think you are the best employee ever! You are always on time and never complain!! You work lots of overtime when needed and I value you on my team!" or "Hey Daryl, I just wanna let you know that you tha fuckin man around here." What should that tell you about my character if anything? What was my excitement/passion level and how could you tell? What does my choice of words say about my education level? What does my choice of words say about my spirituality?

   - You can't tell anything about my character. You can't say I'm a good dad or a bad one; that I'm rich or poor.

- You can tell that my praise level for my employee is high and involves so many different aspects that I know I can say what I said and he would know what it is without me going into a drawn out list.

- You can't tell my level of education by my response.

- You can't tell if I am a Christian or not. Nowhere does it say that there are specific words you should use when giving someone praise or acknowledgement.

4. Special case words: nigga, bitch.. In various parts of the world the word "black" is negro, negru or nero. During the period of African American slavery in America, white people called black people Negroes and the slang term became "nigger". Oddly enough, that term has become a widely accepted term of unification among black people. During slavery, the slave families were all separated and

sold off to different plantations and it became impossible to say the name of the family who you were related to. The only name/term that all blacks had in common was "nigger". Whether you were light or dark complexion, you were equally treated unequally under the law as a "nigger". It has even become a term used by other cultures to mean "homeboy/close friend". Regarding the word "bitch". I know females who use that term on the regular basis as though it's the female version of nigga. At the same time, a man can call that same female a bitch and a fight will break out. Men even use that term with each other and it could be considered a good or bad thing. What should that tell you about my character if anything? What was my excitement/passion level and how could you tell? What does my choice of words say about my education level? What does my choice of words say about my spirituality?

- You can't tell anything about my character. You can't tell whether I'm a good dad or a bad one; whether I'm rich or poor.

- You can tell my passion level only if you understand the pitch and tone when I use that word.

- You can't tell if I dropped out of school or have a Doctor's Degree in Brain Anatomy.

- You can tell nothing about my spirituality when I use that term

5. Business and cuss/slang words is very tricky because in business dealings you have to be aware of cultural differences regarding politics, word choice and a host of other factors to be able to communicate effectively. Example: I have a brother who has a professional service company. When him and I talk or when he talks to black clients, there is one "language" used; but when a white

client comes in, a whole different "language" is used.

Depending on who brings what to the table determines

the language. I have been around important business

meetings where the guy who thought he was in charge

was able to cuss but no one else dared; and I have seen

meetings where nobody cussed…until certain people

walked out the room.

- You can't tell how sharp a person is in business by whether or not he cusses or uses slang. Is a person who refrains from using cuss/slang words until after the meeting better than a person who uses it during a meeting?
- You can't tell his pedigree either.
- You can't tell his spirituality either.

Conclusion: The bottom line is that you can't properly judge a

person by their use or lack of use, of these words. You are not a

better Christian by not using these words. Your segment of a cultural group is no better than another segment of a different

cultural group.

Solutions

- Read the situation before you speak.

- Understand that if you use cuss/slang words
  they may be a barrier to cross cultural
  communication. At the same time, if you don't
  use them, that can also be a barrier to
  communication. In those settings BOTH parties
  should try and understand the other one's use
  of the language.

  - Cuss/slang words convey emotions.
    Emotions can be cultural based and
    complicated. Once you understand the
    emotional impact of words, tread softly...or
    not.

THE POSITIVE EFFECTS OF SLAVERY IN AMERICA

A Christian, African American Male's Perspective

Slavery at its core is not an equally beneficial process for both parties. People who lived through slavery in the United States have, and rightfully so, a stronger emotional connection and reaction to this issue than a student or observer of this topic. For my generation they were just that: stories. For the survivors and the first couple of generations after the "official end of slavery", the heinous stories we read in American history books were their realities and everyday nightmares. This Town Hall Topic discussion is to recognize the effects, positive and negative, that past generations of whites and blacks have had on making America what it is today from a Biblical perspective.

1. American slavery was inflicted upon African Americans by White Americans. True or false?

- If you say true, is it fair to blame and judge the entire White race in America for slavery? If so, how accurate is that assessment?

- If you say false, then is it a more accurate statement to say *some* Whites inflicted American slavery upon African Americans? One could even safely go so far as to say that the majority of White Americans at that time were directly or passively involved with the enforcement of American slavery.

2. I believe it is more accurate to say that *some* White Americans a couple of generations ago were absolutely guilty of supporting that system.

   - Is it the responsibility of the current generation of White Americans to fix it? If yes, what would a practical and implementable solution be?

- If no, then who is responsible to correct past wrongs and what practical steps should be taken to hold the past generation responsible for their behavior?

3. How should Christians view and respond to these issues? What should our focus be? We should do what the Bible says and "seek first the Kingdom of God." This means look at how God acted in substantively similar scenarios in the Bible.

    - Is the Daniel[1] story a good example? In this story, Daniel and the majority of the Israelites were taken into slavery to a foreign country. The end result was that God used slavery as a means to establish His faithful ones to be Governors and visible examples of living a Godly life in the midst of national persecution on foreign soil.

---

[1] Daniel 1

- Is the Joseph[2] story a good example? God allowed
  His faithful Joseph to be sold into slavery by his
  brothers. The end result was that God used slavery
  to elevate His faithful one to Ruler of the land and
  ultimately save that entire country and save the
  Israelites from starving to death during a 7-year
  famine.

- Is the story of how God's chosen people, the
  Israelites, were allowed to remain as slaves in
  Egypt[3] for 400 years a good example? The end
  result was for God to raise up His faithful guy
  Moses as a very visible display of domination and
  leadership over the very powerful Egyptian Empire
  while giving glory to God.

- There is another story of the Israelites being slaves
  and lived on the outskirts in their own little cities

---

2 Genesis 37:26
3 Exodus 1:11

and God instructed them to marry and work with them.

4. What does this tell us we should expect?

- In the Bible, the people taken into slavery ultimately were part of a bigger plan. Is it possible that God used American slavery as a way to raise up His faithful ones in a country that has the resources that those individuals need to operate in to glorify God in front of the whole world?

- America has become the most financially rich country in the world. God needs someone He can trust to control and disperse all this collected wealth properly.

- America has the most powerful military system in the world. God needs someone that He can trust to control this military and use it in a way to protect America AND be the force to protect and serve the unprotected and unserved around the

World.

- America has a political system that when properly

  used gives EVERY person a voice and allows laws to

  be amended and officials elected peacefully. God

  needs someone in charge of this system that He

  can trust to make sure this system does what it's

  designed to do: protect His "garden" and subdue

  it. America's political system has been a

  dominating force in shaping World policies.

5. **Conclusion:** When you focus on the problem the solution

   doesn't get the attention it needs. When you focus on

   payback you can't pay it forward. America is only in this

   position because of the contributions of every cultural

   group that is and that has ever been here. If you were to

   take away or discredit the contributions of any cultural

   group, America's position drops drastically. The most

practical way to correct the past is by correcting your

mentality.

6. **Solutions:**

- Think for yourself: If you form your views based

  on what your cultural group does or should

  be…you are limiting your personal development

  and growth in every area of your life and you can

  be easily swayed, played and manipulated. Look

  at the shift in dollars that sports generate in

  America once players played based on skill level

  instead of cultural group. That shift has created

  wealth and influence that would never have been

  reached if sports stayed the way they were pre

  1970 or so. Politics, business and entertainment

  also all benefitted drastically as a result of

  breaking down cultural barriers.

- Focus on getting yourself in the position where God can put you on the mountaintop and use you. Focus on aligning yourself with other people interested in that. Focus on finding those "diamonds in the rough" that have been overlooked who can help your and God's cause.

- Keep problems in perspective: If a white cop kills a black kid...that simply means a specific white cop killed a specific black kid. It does not mean the entire police force in that city is corrupt. It does not mean black lives don't matter. How comfortable would you feel carrying a sign saying "white lives matter"? That's all a distraction to get people to operate only along cultural lines; while the REAL problem never gets addressed. The real problem is: these shootings primarily happen in areas where residents are not exposed and don't have access to the necessary resources (mentoring, correct spiritual teaching, financial, job opportunities) to make their communities places where there is no need for strong police presence.

- Consistently support a local mentoring program with your time or money. Consistently support local agencies that actively help residents become employable AND connect them to employers on a regular basis. You and some friends create support groups for young people or single parents or whatever you have a passion for.

- Consistently make choices that allow you to do your passion and be the best Christian/person you can be. Your life choices determine your level of usefulness in Kingdom work AND your passion and purpose in life. You may not have money to support a local cause because you spend it partying on the weekends. You may make sexual choices that go against the Bible and now you find yourself a single parent feeling like you HAVE to work two jobs and hustle and you deserve to party on the weekend as an escape. We have shifted our focus to "Nobody can judge me because I'm taking care of me and my kids and working two jobs and paying my rent and car note" and there is rightfully a sense of pride in that; but what would happen if we focused on saying "I've been making choices that are from the Bible and I've been able to have a car and a house and a job and help other people?"

A book without about fighting and wars without talking about America's war on drug would be an incomplete book. I mentioned to you in this book that God is a God of war and that if you are going to fight a war and claim that God supports you, you had better make sure God knows about your efforts or you will fail.

The bullshit American "War on Drugs" is one of those wars that claimed to be sanctioned by God Himself, but was no more than an all-out attack on black American citizens by the then all-white-male controlled congress, military and local police officers.

Some of you might stop reading because you may be thinking, "Oh boy, here he goes on some political rambling or black inequality stuff…" but that's not it. Keep reading and you will see how I tie America's "drug war" with God and war.

America has always claimed they are supported and loved by God. American currency says "In God we trust". The American national anthem says, "...God bless America..." When an American President or judge swears into office, he or she has to put a hand on the Bible and swear to fulfill the duties of the office "...so help me God..."

You would think American policies are based on God with all the God references. If you think that your ass is wrong as two left shoes.

When slavery ended in America, millions of African Americans were denied access to legal employment. One of the best options to create the most wealth soon became selling drugs. Large shipments of drugs were not brought into the poor, black communities by black people. White people with links to American government agencies like the FBI, CIA as well as Columbian and Mexican drug traffickers get the credit for those deliveries.

Even though rich, white Americans and everyday white Americans were both selling tons of cocaine and getting high at huge parties and spending billions of dollars a year on powder cocaine, aka blow, America wasn't thinking about declaring war just yet. The Italian gangsters were making millions off the drug trade without much attention from the American government. It wasn't until African Americans began to make money and create gangs to protect drug turfs that America decided to "wage a war against drugs because drugs is America's public enemy #1" all of a sudden.

How does this tie in to God and war? Since America claims to have the backing and support of God in its' financial, national and political arenas, if it declares war, by its' very nature it must be supported by God.

This is where America fucked up and began to split itself down the middle based on skin color and show its' true colors. You can't use military weaponry, personnel and military grade armored vehicles, local police officers and corrupt legislation tied

directly to corrupt prison systems and sentencing and expect to

have the support of God.

I told you God loves war. What America did was it got prideful

and decided it could wage war however the fuck it wanted to and

God would bless it.

God loves war when it is used to establish Heaven on Earth.

That means, war is sanctioned by God to protect and value the

lives of human beings through sound political and financial

practices. America disgraced itself before God and is now paying

the price.

The opiate or opioid "crisis" has recently emerged in America

and is ravaging white communities. These drugs are medically

prescribed daily through hospitals and med-centers all across

America illegally...and nobody in politics wants to declare war.

This drug situation has called for America to spend billions of dollars, not in war and attacking hospitals and others linked to the sale of opiates, but for rehabilitation. This drug that is killing white America is not a drug that is worthy of American warfare. It is a drug problem that is apparently worthy of America's need to come together and help those with opiate addictions. Treat them with love and kindness. Support those whose family members have died from this addiction.

I don't mean to be callous or cold but I call bullshit when I see it. If America wants to truly be a nation that fights for what is right and truly wants the support of God as we claim to have, we better stop letting a bunch of racist-ass bitches control our social and political policies and start waging war the way God designed it.

I'm not even mad that America has chosen to kill, attack and criminalize drugs when it was in the black community and has chosen to treat drugs that affect the white community with love, peace and understanding. Black people saw America's reaction

coming a mile away and weren't surprised at all.

What I am saying with this Private Matter essay is that war is

and can be a good thing when used properly and when it is truly

sanctioned by God. Since I have wrapped my noodle around the

fact that human-sanctioned war will continue to be based on

greed, prejudice and corruption, I have been able to change my

focus.

I now can truly say I am involved in warfare that is sanctioned

by God. How can I say that? I can tell you upfront that it has

absolutely nothing to do with being an American citizen or any

type of American, "God bless America" bumper sticker, "In God

we trust" bullshit.

No, I have signed up for spiritual warfare. This warfare has

morals. This warfare has real objectives that are designed to both create equality among humans and support the work that Jesus started for us when He was on Earth.

I no longer give a fuck about America's dishonorable and disgustingly racist "war on drugs" in the black community. In the same vein, I no longer care that America chose not to wage war on white drug activity.

I am able to wage war against real enemies like Satan, political corruption, homosexual activity, financial market scams and other major causes of chaos in our societies. I am able to access physical and spiritual weaponry and resources in this quest. I truly have the backing of God Himself when I enter the battlefield and it feels good!!!

The Bible Fight Club is looking for people who really want to fight for some really good causes. If that's you, study the Bible, understand what your ass is about to get in to, study God's war tactics and strategies and prepare to fight for causes that are free

of racism, greed, corruption and sin.

Welcome to the Bible Fight Club, fellow warrior!!!

B.I.B.L.E.

(Basic Instructions Before Leaving Earth)

Personal Development Notes

Personal Development Notes

Personal Development Notes

Personal Development Notes